Beautiful
Montana
Vol. II

Beautiful
Montana
Vol. II

Text by Rick Graetz

First Printing July 1979

ISBN 0-89802-006-9
ISBN 0-89802-005-0 (paperback)

Published by Beautiful America Publishing Company
P.O. Box 608, Beaverton, Oregon 97005
Robert D. Shangle, Publisher

PHOTO CREDITS

BOB CLEMENZ—*pages 16-17; page 46; pages 48-49.*

ED COOPER—*pages 12-13; pages 60-61; pages 64-65.*

LAWRENCE B. DODGE—*page 57; page 69, below.*

RICK GRAETZ—*page 15; page 20; page 21; page 22; page 23; page 24; page 36; page 37; page 40; page 41; page 43, below; page 47, above; page 50, below; page 53; page 54; page 56; page 57, below; page 68, above; page 69, above.*

PAT O' HARA—*page 9; pages 32-33; pages 44-45; page 51; page 52.*

MICHAEL B. SAMPLES—*page 10; page 11, below; page 14; page 19; page 42; page 47, below; page 68, above.*

ROBERT D. SHANGLE—*page 18, above.*

GUS WOLFE—*page 50, above; page 55, above.*

Enlarged Prints

Most of the photography
in this book is available as
photographic enlargements.
Send self-addressed, stamped
envelope for information.
Beautiful America Publishing Company
P.O. Box 608
Beaverton, Oregon 97005

Send $1.00 for complete catalog
Beautiful America Publishing Company
P.O. Box 608
Beaverton, Oregon 97005

CONTENTS

Beautiful America Publishing Company

The nation's foremost publisher of quality color photography

CURRENT BOOKS

Alaska, Arizona, British Columbia, California, California Vol. II, California Coast, California Desert, California Missions, Colorado, Florida, Georgia, Hawaii, Los Angeles, Idaho, Illinois, Maryland, Michigan, Michigan Vol. II, Minnesota, Montana, Montana Vol. II, Mt. Hood (Oregon), New York, New Mexico, Northern California, Northern California Vol. II, North Idaho, Oregon, Oregon Vol. II, Oregon Coast, Oregon Mountains, Portland, Pennsylvania, San Diego, San Francisco, Texas, Utah, Washington, Washington Vol. II, Washington, D.C., Wisconsin, Yosemite National Park.

FORTHCOMING BOOKS

California Mountains, Indiana, Kentucky, Las Vegas, Massachusetts, Mississippi, Missouri, Nevada, New Jersey, North Carolina, Oklahoma, Ozarks, Rocky Mountains, San Juan Islands, Seattle, South Carolina, Tennessee, Vermont, Wyoming.

LARGE FORMAT, HARDBOUND BOOKS

Beautiful America, Beauty of California, Glory of Nature's Form, Lewis & Clark Country, Western Impressions.

Send $1.00 for complete catalog
Beautiful America Publishing Company
Robert D. Shangle, Publisher
Post Office Box 608
Beaverton, Oregon 97005

Copyright © 1979

PROLOGUE

The photography in this book depicts some of Montana's designated wilderness areas, *de facto* wilderness regions and, in general, roadless and semi-roadless wild areas found on the prairie and in the mountains.

Wilderness and wild areas are among Montana's greatest assets. They represent the epitome of multiple use of our national forest lands. These areas protect watersheds and wildlife habitat, creating havens for fish and wildlife—a sportsman's paradise. They open up vast acreage to people of all ages and income levels who are taking part in one of the fastest-growing recreational uses of the national forests today: wilderness recreation. It's a high quality form of recreation that people can enjoy without spending lots of money.

These aesthetic values are not the only benefits of wilderness. It also has great economic value to the state. Tourists are attracted to it for its beauty and unspoiled landscape, making tourism Montana's third largest industry. Wilderness affords watershed protection for agriculture, the state's number one industry. Outdoor equipment businesses are growing fast, owing to the ready market for their wares. Although one cannot put a monetary value on life quality, it is part of the economic picture as well, and undeveloped country adds greatly to the quality of life in Montana.

Because of Montana's vastness, the millions of acres of wilderness and undeveloped country represent only a small portion of the state's total area. Yet within these solitary expanses exists a striking variety of landforms and vegetation: rugged mountains, lakes, forests and rivers, prairies and badlands are all represented in the state's borders.

Wilderness, and de facto wilderness, is very accessible, and this book has been designed as an introduction to the variety of the backcountry. It's not necessary to shoulder a heavy pack and trudge off to spend weeks in solitary communion with the mountains . . . all it really takes to experience the beauty and solitude of Montana is the urge to stop the car once in a while, get out and look around. A day's hike, a horseback ride, or a drive to the end of the road can put anyone, regardless of physical condition or age, in touch with enough wild beauty to soothe his spirit, and restore his priorities and sensitivity to the value of wild country.

To be sure, this writer is prejudiced towards undeveloped land. I've seen the ill effects of developing all available open space. The knowledge that large tracts of land exist and are accessible, unscarred by roads and development, can't help adding to the good life for all people . . . not just Montanans. Fortunately, more and more people are discovering that wild lands and designated wilderness are a priceless and a worthwhile commodity; a commodity that does not detract from a healthy economy, but rather enhances the economic well-being of an area.

This book is frankly an attempt to win you over. It is a portfolio of scenic photography of some of Montana's most beautiful country. Then, to tempt you to go out and look for yourself, the text has been organized as a series of tours that will get you out into beautiful country for as much or as little time as you have to spend. I hope that this book, both pictures and text, will entice readers to discover the value of Montana's undeveloped lands on their own—and preserve its beauty for those that follow.

Rick Graetz

INTRODUCTION

Montana is a big, rugged, and sparsely-settled state. That's a fact that bodes well for Montanans, and people in general, especially those who love to meet nature in its wild and unspoiled form. The relatively small amount of tampering man has done with the landscape has left a large amount of Montana free, wild and open—a haven for lovers of beautiful scenery. And what scenery! Mountains, forests, wild rivers, lakes, prairies, badlands and deserts—Montana has it all.

What's more, from the mountain country of the west to the prairie lands of the east—and everything in between—the scenery of Montana is easily accessible. Those who enjoy hiking have millions of acres of designated wilderness available, and a surprising amount of country is accessible to those who wish to see Montana by car. The hiker or driver needs only to choose what he wants to see, and plan accordingly.

The traveler who is interested in high country has choices scattered all over the map. The Absaroka-Beartooth region features the highest peaks in Montana, a vast expanse of tundra and arctic-like terrain, countless lakes, glaciers and waterfalls. This scenery, including the perimeters of the Absaroka-Beartooth Wilderness, is accessible by car via the spectacular Beartooth Highway, a road winding from Red Lodge on the east to Cooke City on the west. At Cooke City it links up with the roads of Yellowstone National Park.

Up near the International Border, the backcountry of Glacier National Park and the Mission Mountain Wilderness area present some of the most beautiful scenery anywhere in Montana. The backcountry contains glacial-scoured terrain, lakes, waterfalls and an abundance of wildlife. Going to the Sun Highway offers the same vistas to motorists over Logan Pass in Glacier National Park and on the Swan Valley Highway between Bigfork and Clearwater Junction.

The Madison and Gallatin Ranges of southwestern Montana present mountain terrain that differs from the Glacier and Beartooth regions. The country is higher than that found in the Missions and Glacier, yet somewhat lower than the alpine tundra of the Beartooth. The Gallatin Canyon Road between Bozeman and West Yellowstone, and the Madison Valley Highway between Harrison and Quake Lake, offer a view of scenery that the backcountry traveler finds along the mountain trails.

The Cabinet Mountains and Wilderness Area of northwestern Montana feature some of the greatest relief found in Montana, as well as some of the richest

(Third preceding page) Arnica grows close to the pool beneath Trick Falls, in Glacier National Park.

(Second preceding page) The bighorn ram is found in Montana's high and wild country.

(Preceding page, above) Lupine dots the open sage range country west of White Sulphur Springs. Mt. Edith rises in the distance.

(Preceding page, below) This is the north face of Granite Peak, Montana's highest point at 12,799 feet. Glacier Peak is in the background.

(Left) St. Mary Lake is already in shadow and the moon has risen, while the slanting rays of the afternoon sun touch the peaks with light in Glacier National Park.

(Following page) Cottonwoods and aspens show off their magnificent autumn colors on the banks of Rock Creek, which flows out of the Beartooth Mountains near Red Lodge.

(Second following page, above) Late June often brings thunder storms to the prairie regions of Montana, stacking up thunderheads like this one, photographed near the Powder River crossing east of Miles City.

(Second following page, below) Upriver from Judith Landing, the Missouri River flows past rugged rock formations in the white rocks country.

(Preceding pages) Grinnell Peak looms over the waters of Swiftcurrent Lake in Glacier National Park.

(Left) Montana gardens reward the efforts of rose fanciers with blooms like these.

(Below) Koch Peak is in the Taylor Peaks section of southwestern Montana, in the Madison Range.

(Opposite) An inquisitive grizzly cub sizes up the photographer, who maintained a respectful distance by using a telephoto lens for this shot.

(Following page) Ross Creek meanders through the Giant Cedars area, where heavy snowfall and spring rains create the rain-forest conditions the big trees require.

(Preceding page, above) The first snows of autumn have already dusted the northern end of the Swan Range, near Kalispell, with white.

(Preceding page, below) The Powder River, north of Broadus, is frequently described as being ''a mile wide and a foot deep'' as it makes its way across the isolated Montana prairies.

(Left) Indian Paintbrush blooms through Montana's western mountain regions, on both sides of the continental divide.

(Below) Windmill and cabin still stand on this abandoned homestead in the Powder River country.

(Opposite) This view is from the Rimrocks, southeast of Billings, looking toward the Pryor Mountains.

(Following page, above) This central Montana ghost town testifies to the rigorous lives of early settlers in this rugged country. Not all met with success.

(Following page, below) This Mission Mountain creek nourishes a variety of wildflowers on its wild tumble down the slopes.

vegetation. Giant cedar trees and dense forests offer the backpacker a totally different kind of terrain. The road through the Bull River country between Noxon and Libby offers similar scenery to the motorist, and it's possible to drive to the perimeter of the giant cedar trees.

The Pioneer Mountains, the Beaverhead Range and the west Big Hole country offer yet more escapes to the wilderness for the back country traveler. Towering peaks, lakes and beautiful mountain meadows are the rule in this country. Roads cross the Wise River country, bisecting the Pioneer Range, exploring the length of the Big Hole Valley, and opening some of the lake regions of the west Big Hole.

Not really mountainous but still spectacular, the Missouri River Breaks and the wild Missouri River offer open prairie, broken by deep river canyons and spectacular cliffs. It's good country for hiking or float trips. For those wishing to see the same type of scenery by automobile, several roads breach the Missouri River region. There is a road from Big Sandy to Judith Landing, and others stretch into the Breaks from the Fred Robinson Bridge north of Lewistown, and south of Malta, and Coalbanks Landing north of Fort Benton. Motorists may also enter the Charles M. Russell Wildlife Refuge on Fort Peck Lake, on a road east from Fred Robinson Bridge, or one from Jordan to Hell's Creek.

Montana's designated wilderness areas add a whole new dimension for the explorer of the high-and-wild country. Even the names sound exciting. Consider the Bob Marshall Wilderness, the Scapegoat Wilderness, the Great Bear Wilderness, the Cabinet Mountains Wilderness, the Mission Mountain Wilderness, the Selway-Bitterroot Wilderness, the Welcome Creek Wilderness, the Spanish Peaks Primitive Area, the Absaroka-Beartooth Wilderness and the Gates of the Mountains Wilderness. And there are more areas under consideration that will add to the list. To list the access sites and describe the thousands of miles of trails would take another book. Luckily, information on all of Montana's wilderness areas is available from the Region 1 Headquarters of the U.S. Forest Service in Missoula (zip code 59801).

Of course, even better than knowing about wilderness is the chance to get out into it. Many areas accessible by motor vehicle offer outstanding scenery, photographic opportunities, and other recreation: all it takes is knowing where to

(Preceding page) Mt. Grinnell rises sharply behind the blue waters of Grinnell Lake, high in Glacier National Park.

start. With just a little knowledge of the kinds of scenery in the state, and a road map, it is possible to plan trips to fit the individual budget, schedule, and taste.

Briefly, Montana's scenic areas may be divided into six distinct regions.

Northwestern Montana

This in an area of heavy precipitation, dense forest land and magnificent mountain peaks. Deep river canyons, rather than broad valleys, are the rule in this region.

Southwestern Montana

This region holds high, broad, sagebrush-covered river valleys and mountain peaks somewhat higher than found in northwestern Montana. The highest peaks in southwestern Montana exceed 11,000 feet. The forests in the southwest aren't as dense, owing to drier conditions. Both areas offer outstanding fishing.

North-Central Montana

This region extends east from the Rocky Mountains to Lewistown and to Helena on the south. It features some of Montana's isolated mountain ranges such as the Sweetgrass Hills, the Highwoods, the Bearpaw Mountains, the Judiths and the Little Rockies. The wild Missouri River drains a portion of this area. Wheat fields and river canyons dominate the scenery.

South-Central Montana

This region boasts of big valleys, rather than prairie, and Montana's most spectacular mountains, the Crazy Mountains, Bridger Range and the Beartooth Mountains, with peaks ranging as high as 12,709 feet. Bozeman is the westernmost boundary and Billings is the eastern point. Southcentral Montana also features the state's only desert region, south and west of the Pryor Mountains. Although not as dry as the deserts of the southwestern United States, the area is nonetheless desertlike in appearance.

(Left) A breeze ripples the surface of Goose Lake, and cloud shadows drift across the face of the Sawtooth Peaks, in the Beartooth Mountains.

Northeastern Montana

This is a region of wide open country and badlands. Fort Peck Lake, a beautiful body of water with more than 1,600 miles of shoreline, is one of the dominant features of northeast Montana. The lake is bordered by the C.M. Russell Wildlife Refuge, one of many in this section of the state along US Highway 2.

Southeastern Montana

Like northeastern Montana, this is wide open country, perhaps the state's most remote. Southeastern Montana features the magnificent Powder River region, the Medicine Rocks and Chalk Buttes near Ekalaka. The free-flowing Yellowstone River drains southeastern Montana.

To help the traveler, we'd like to suggest a few trips through this diverse landscape.

Southeast Montana

Trip #1: Miles City—Ekalaka—Powderville—Broadus

This trip takes in the extreme southeast area of Montana, offering some of the finest scenery the region has to offer: big, open range, badlands, buttes, strange rock formations and the fabled Powder River.

The starting point is Miles City. Follow US 12 east toward Baker. Enroute you will cross the Powder River, and pause to climb some of the bluffs above the river. From Baker, head south on State Highway 7 to Ekalaka, a distance of about 35 miles. In this region is Medicine Rocks State Park, and portions of the Custer National Forest (southeast of Ekalaka and near the South Dakota state line). Southwest of Ekalaka, a secondary road leads to the Chalk Buttes area. You can follow the road to Powderville, seat of the Powder River country, and then continue northwest to Highway 312, which connects Broadus and Miles City. If you have some extra time, don't cross the river at Powderville—instead, head south on the gravel road to the town of Broadus. From there you can pick up Highway 312 and drive back to Miles City. The trip can be done in as few as two days, or as many as five.

Trip #2: Billings—Bighorn Canyon—Busby— Lame Deer—Colstrip

The area south and east of Billings offers some of Montana's most unusual scenery. From Billings, follow Interstate Highway 90 east to Hardin; then turn off on Secondary Route 313 south to Fort Smith and Big Horn Canyon National Recreation Area. The Big Horn River at this point has been dammed by Yellowtail Dam, and might be called Montana's Grand Canyon. The area to the west of Big Horn Canyon is called the Pryor Mountains, and to the south is Montana's desert land. The Pryor Mountains contain ice caves and are home for wild horses. From Fort Smith head back on Highway 313, turning off to Crow Agency and the Custer Battlefield National Monument. This is your chance to walk through the battlefield of General George Custer's Last Stand and down along the valley of the Little Big Horn. The mountains just to the south of the Custer Battlefield are called the Rosebud Mountains. From the Custer Battlefield, drive east on US Highway 212 to Busby and Lame Deer, on the Northern Cheyenne Indian Reservation. The country

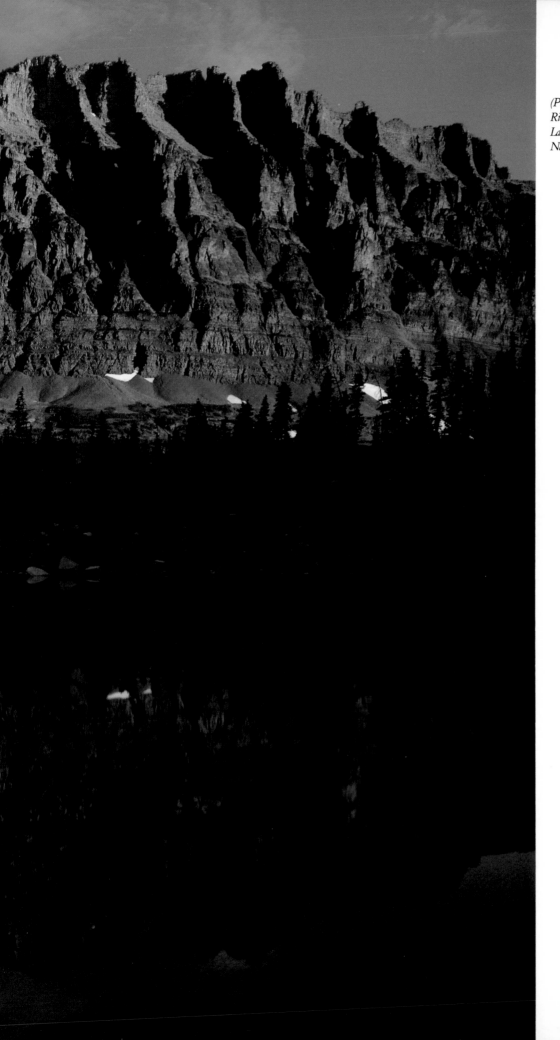

(Preceding page) Mt. Rockwell and Sinopah Ridge reflect in the still waters of Cobalt Lake in an early morning view in Glacier National Park.

offers diverse scenery, from open prairie to forested land. There are many high points offering outstanding views of the surrounding countryside. Just east of Lame Deer and outside of the reservation, one can drive through parts of the Custer National Forest. This would make an interesting side trip and you might consider a stop in Ashland, the site of the St. Labre School for Indians. Coming back to Lame Deer, drive north on Secondary Route 315 to Colstrip, Montana. Here you will have an opportunity to view the strip mining operations. From Colstrip keep going north on Highway 15 back to Interstate 94 just to the west of Forsyth. The road then continues back towards Billings along the Yellowstone River. A worthwhile stop is at Pompey's Pillar, an historic site where Lewis and Clark carved their names in a rock. A person should take a minimum of two days to make this trip and perhaps three. It is worth the time to camp in the area of Big Horn Canyon. Campsites are also available on the Northern Cheyenne Indian Reservation and the Custer National Forest.

Northeast Montana

Trip #1: Fort Peck Lake
Charles M. Russell Wildlife Refuge

This is a long trip through big country. Fort Peck Lake is the dominant feature, with more than 1,600 miles of shoreline bounded by Charles M. Russell Wildlife Refuge, a region of badland scenery, buttes, magnificent vistas of the lake and the Missouri River Breaks. Starting from Lewiston, take Highway 191 to the Fred Robinson Bridge, where camping is available and roads lead into the Wildlife Refuge. North along Highway 191 to Malta, a side trip may be taken through the semi-ghost towns of Landusky or Zortman, in the isolated Little Rocky Mountains. From Malta, Highway 2 leads east to Glasgow. En route, several wildlife refuges are open to the public. Highway 24 then crosses the dam and runs south where it meets Highway 200, east of Jordan. Along this route roads again lead into the Russell Wildlife Refuge and Fort Peck Lake. Some of Montana's finest badland scenery is visible along this highway. From Jordan, Highway 200 runs west, back to Lewistown. This trip has the best scenery eastern Montana has to offer and is very worthwhile for the photographer. You can make the trip in as little as two or three days, but it is better to take five or six days, or even a week if you have it.

Trip #2: Glasgow—Fort Peck Lake—Circle—
Culbertson—Scobey

This trip begins at Glasgow and gives the traveler an opportunity to view a portion of Fort Peck Lake and some of the rolling hill country of northeastern Montana. From Glasgow drive southeast on State Highway 24 to the town of Fort Peck and Fort Peck Dam. You might enjoy camping in one of the many campgrounds near the lake, or motel accommodations are available in Fort Peck. For a side trip, drive farther south on Highway 24 to the Bear Creek or Rock Creek Recreation Areas, then continue south on Highway 24, turning east on US 200 to the town of Circle. This region offers a close-up view of some of Montana's wildest badlands.

(Following page, above) Winter in the Swan Valley brings a blanket of snow to the Swan Range and the valley floor.
(Following page, below) The Medicine Rocks country north of Ekalaka. This is an area of strange sandstone rocks, etched out by wind action and freezing and thawing. The area is most colorful during the months of June and July.

From Circle head north on Highway 13 to Wolf Point, a major town on the Fort Peck Indian Reservation. At Wolf Point, go east on US Highway 2 along the Missouri River to the town of Culbertson.

From Culbertson take a side trip for a few miles on Highway 16 toward Plentywood. Midway between the two towns is the Medicine Lake National Wildlife Refuge, a worthwhile stop. North of Plentywood turn west on Highway 5 toward Scobey, a town just south of the Canadian line which offers some very unusual scenery. A replica of a pioneer town and museum is situated outside the town as well. It is popular with visitors. From Scobey, drive south on Highway 13 back to US 2 just east of Wolf Point, and from there, take Highway 2 back to Glasgow. To get the most out of this area, it is a good idea to spend one night at Fort Peck and perhaps another in Wolf Point. You can then make the loop to Scobey, stay overnight there, and make the drive back to Glasgow the next day. This would be the leisurely way to see the area, and would guarantee time for good photography.

(Preceding page, above) Autumn comes early to the banks of the Boulder River, sometimes turning the leaves to red and gold in late August or early September.
(Preceding page, below) Cliff Lake, an isolated lake in the Mission Mountains, holds its ice well into July and sometimes barely thaws out before the heavy snows of winter seal the country closed again.

South-Central Montana

Trip #1: Red Lodge—The Beartooth Highway— Cooke City

This route, extending from Red Lodge, Montana on the east to Cooke City, Montana on the west crosses through the roof of Montana. The highway reaches an elevation of 10,940 feet at Beartooth Pass. The distance of the trip is approximately 65 miles, but there are so many side trips via short walks that it is advisable to plan on doing some camping on this trip. The towering peaks of the Beartooth Mountains are visible and one will have the opportunity to cross tundra and snow fields interspersed with wildflowers and lakes.

Trip #2: Bozeman—Wilsall—Crazy Mountains— Harlowton—Big Timber

A short but worthwhile trip starts at Bozeman, Montana, following Secondary Route 293 along the Bridger Range toward Bridger Bowl Ski Area. The road is gravel surfaced in places as it goes north and eventually comes out just north of Wilsall. East of Highway 89, the route leads into the Crazy Mountains. It would make a worthwhile side trip. From the junction at Highway 89, drive to Ringling and then four miles north, turning east on Highway 294. You will be driving through open sage country with the Castle Mountains on the north side and the Crazy Mountains to the south. The road climbs high and offers magnificent vistas of the surrounding broad valleys and high mountain ranges. You should plan some time here to get out and do some exploring and photography. Two miles north of Martinsdale, Highway 294 meets US 12. Turn east toward Harlowton, passing the town of Two Dot, and drive along the valley of the Musselshell River. The Crazy Mountains still will be in sight on the south and the mountains to the north are the Little Belts. Far in the distance to the northeast you'll be able to see the Big Snowy Mountains. Go through Harlowton on US 191, south toward Big Timber. North of Big Timber, a road goes

(Following page, above) In the heart of the Bob Marshall Wilderness Area, the limestone escarpment of the Chinese Wall tilts its face to the east.
(Following page, below) Black Angus cattle huddle against the 40-below cold of a Montana prairie winter.

(Third preceding page) Mt. Villard, the Sawtooth Spires and Granite Peak are reflected in the smooth waters of Rough Lake, in the Beartooth Mountains.

(Second preceding page) Ptarmigan rest in the snow.

(Preceding page, above) Thunderheads boil up behind this lake in the Madison Range.

(Preceding page, below) Sunset seems to turn the Missouri River to fire at Coal Banks Landing, downstream from Fort Benton.

(Left) The sun rises over the continental divide to highlight Prairie Reef in the Bob Marshall Wilderness Area.

(Following page) The Garden Wall provides a backdrop for a field of Glacier Lilies in Glacier National Park.

(Second following page, above) The Rocky Mountain front stretches northward in this view from a prairie butte near Great Falls.

(Second following page, below) The Crazy Mountains, already powdered with snow after the wheat harvest, rise behind this stubblefield in the Shields River Valley.

(Preceding pages) Snow melt from Mt. Reynolds keeps this stream running year around in the Hanging Gardens, Glacier National Park.

(Left) A mountain goat surveys his precipitous domain.

(Below) The west end of the Spanish Peaks, southwest of Bozeman, looks like this from the top of Andesite Mountain.

(Opposite) Rosy spirea graces the shores of Upper Geiger Lake, in the Cabinet Mountains Wilderness.

(Following page) Penstemon wildflowers brighten a rocky slope in Glacier National Park, while the rugged peak of Bearhat Mountain rises in the background.

(Second following page, above) Echo Peak (11,200 feet) is on the right, and the pointed peak in the background center is Hilgard Peak, at 11,300 feet the highest in the Madison Range.

(Second following page, below) This wintry scene was captured in the Beartooth Mountains north of Cooke City. This portion of the Beartooths borders Yellowstone National Park.

(Opposite, above) East of Fort Peck Lake and northeast of Jordan, some of Montana's finest badlands scenery presents its forbidding face.

(Opposite, below) An early winter storm moves across the prairie. In some such storms, as much as three feet of snow have been blown into North Dakota, and chill factors have reached 50 degrees below zero.

(Right) Inquisitive coyote pups stand among prairie wildflowers.

(Below) Verdant growth fills the bottomlands in the Rock Creek Area north of Hinsdale, while drier conditions prevail on the hillsides.

(Following page, above) As winter's snow continue to melt from the mountains, hardy wildflowers line the shores of this lake in the Madison Range.

(Following page, below) This wintry view of the Bitterroot Mountains is from Miner Lake Road, in the Big Hole Valley.

into the Crazy Mountains toward Half Moon Campground. This would be a great place to camp overnight and start a day-hike along some of the trails of the Crazy Mountains. Coming back on 191, go to the town of Big Timber and then head west on Interstate 90 back to Bozeman. This trip can be made in one day if you start early in the morning, but a weekend would allow you to camp out and view some of the Crazy Mountains.

(Preceding page, above) The Yellowstone River looks peaceful as it flows through Paradise Valley, with the peaks of the North Absaroka Range rising behind.
(Preceding page, below) Pelicans raise their young on Pelican Island in the Bowdoin Wildlife Refuge near Malta.

North-Central Montana

Trip #1: The Rocky Mountain Front

The eastern front of the Rockies, from Glacier Park on the north to Augusta on the south, offers the traveler a view of the escarpment of the Rocky Mountains where it meets the rolling prairie. The starting point can be either East Glacier Park or Augusta, Montana. Highways 287 and 89 are the main routes. Many side roads lead into the Rocky Mountain Front, and one of the best routes is up the Teton River out of Choteau. This route gives the traveler an opportunity to drive over one of the passes of the Rocky Mountain Front and into some of the river regions. Also a route out of Augusta leads into Gibson Lake and makes a loop, returning to Augusta.

Trip #2: Great Falls—Bearpaw Mountains— The Little Rockies

Starting from Great Falls, this trip offers very diverse eastern Montana scenery, including isolated mountain ranges, the wild Missouri River and the historic Fort Belknap Indian Reservation. Drive from Great Falls north on US 87, and take the side road off of 87 into the town of Fort Benton. Fort Benton has been called the birthplace of Montana and was the head of steam navigation on the Missouri. The town is historic and picturesque. From Fort Benton, drive north to Big Sandy on Highway 87, then follow secondary routes to Warwick and Cleveland. Warwick is a single old building, and Cleveland is a semi-ghost town. This is a secondary route, but the gravel roads make good driving in dry weather. The best time to drive this route is in June or July, to catch sight of green grass and blooming prairie flowers. This is the vicinity of the Bear Paw Mountains, another of Montana's unusual isolated prairie mountain ranges. From Cleveland, drive north on Secondary Route 240, passing the Chief Joseph Battleground and State Monument, where Chief Joseph surrendered to the U.S. Cavalry when he was trying to flee into Canada. From Chief Joseph Battleground, drive north to Chinook, turning east on US 2 to Harlem and the Fort Belknap Agency. Highway 376 goes south along the Little Rocky Mountains and through the Fort Belknap Indian Reservation. If you have a four-wheel-drive vehicle or pickup truck, a road crosses the Little Rocky Mountains at Hayes and emerges at Landusky. In places the road is rough and it is not advisable to

59

(Left) Indian Paintbrush brightens the slope above Grinnell Lake in this Glacier National Park scene.

take a car over it, so if you're using an automobile, continue north on 376 to the Landusky turnoff. From there you can drive the short distance to the semi-ghost town of Landusky and view some of the old mines and historic sights. The Little Rocky Mountains are steeped in history and Landusky was the hangout of many outlaws, including Kid Curry and his gang. A possible side trip can be made by coming back out on Highway 376 to the junction with US 191, and driving a short distance north to the Zortman turnoff on Highway 191, toward Malta. Zortman is a very colorful town and the Little Rocky Mountains generally slope upward from this point and offer beautiful vistas of the surrounding prairie and forested hills. At the 376 and 191 junction, drive south to the Fred Robinson Bridge and the Missouri River crossing. At this point there are some side roads leading into the Charles M. Russell National Wildlife Refuge and the James Kipp Recreation Area. This is a great place for photographers, because the area is home to much wildlife. This is also an ideal place to view the Missouri River Breaks country. You are well advised to camp overnight in this region. If you have a canoe you can float the Missouri River into the Wildlife Refuge for a distance.

From this point, drive south on US 191 along the the Judith and Moccasin Mountains. Another interesting side trip is the drive toward the ghost town of Maiden in the heart of the Judith Mountains. If you have time, drive up north to the higher points of the Judith Mountains where you may look out over the prairie. Coming back to Highway 191, drive south to Lewistown and then west on US 87 back to Great Falls.

In taking this trip, one should plan on camping in the Bear Paw Mountains or at least staying overnight in the town of Chinook to have a look at the Bear Paw Mountains. It would be worthwhile to spend another night camped in the vicinity of the Little Rocky Mountains or preferably at the James Kipp Recreation Area. Landusky and Zortman and the Little Rocky Mountains have campgrounds as does the James Kipp area.

Northwest Montana

Trip #1: Cabinet Mountains and Bull River

Northwestern Montana, the Cabinet Mountain Country, the Bull River area and the Thompson River offer great mountain and forest scenery and the highest contours to be found in the state. The starting point for this trip is Thompson Falls, on Highway 200. From Thompson Falls, head north on Highway 200 along the Clark Fork to Noxon. On the west side, the Bitterroot Mountains rise in the distance, forming the Montana-Idaho border, and the Cabinet Mountains are on the east side. Just north of Noxon, turn on State Highway 202 through the Bull River country. Here you will have a chance to visit the Ross Creek giant cedar trees area and view beautiful Bull Lake and the towering peaks of the Cabinet Mountains. The altitude in this area ranges to over 6,000 feet. Make sure you have plenty of film while in the Bull River area. Stay north on highway 202 to meet US 2 just west of Libby. Toward Libby, you will have a chance to take a side trip to the beautiful Lake Kookanusa; beyond Libby, head east on US 2 to vicinity of Logan Recreation Area and Thompson Lake. Here a secondary gravel road crosses the range along the Thompson River and comes out just a few miles east of Thompson Falls on Highway 200. You can continue along Highway 2 to Kalispell, and then south on US 93 along Flathead Lake to State Highway 28 at Elmo. Highway 28 then crosses through the Hot Springs area and comes out on Highway 200.

Trip #2: Mission Mountains—Swan Valley

This trip offers the spectacular escarpment of the Mission Mountain Range and magnificent Swan Valley. From Missoula, head west on US 10 to a junction with US 93. Drive north on US 93 to the town of St. Ignatius, on the Flathead Indian Reservation. From St. Ignatius, you can take a short side trip to the Mission Reservoir, which brings you right up against the sheer wall of the Mission Mountain Range; or drive north to the town of Polson on Flathead Lake. From Polson, turn north on US 93 on the west shore of Flathead Lake. Highway 35 skirts the lake on the east side, but the best views of Flathead Lake and the mountains are seen from the west side. Following Highway 93 north, just beyond the turnoff to Somers, go east on

(Left) This is the view from Devils Canyon Overlook in the Bighorn Canyon National Wilderness Area.

Secondary Road 208 toward Bigfork, to the junction of US 35. Head south on 35 a short distance into Bigfork, a colorful town and home of a well-known summer playhouse. Just one mile south of Bigfork is the turnoff to Secondary Highway 209. Follow 209 south toward the town of Swan Lake and the route to the beautiful Swan Valley. On your west will be the other side of the Mission Mountain Range and wilderness area, and on your east the skyward-reaching escarpment of the Swan Range, the western boundary of the famous Bob Marshall Wilderness Area. There are many Forest Service campgrounds throughout the Swan Valley, and Montana highway maps mark these clearly. Both the Swan and Flathead Valleys offer magnificent sights for photographers. Follow Highway 209 to its end at US 200, at Clearwater Junction, then go west on Highway 200 and back to Missoula. This trip should take a minimum of two days, and preferably three. Ideally you could stay overnight in the town of Bigfork and take in a play, and then continue for a leisurely drive the next day halfway through the Swan Valley, camping out at one of the many campgrounds. One of the best is in the Holland Lake area, halfway through the valley. This route is also famous for a yearly bicycle tour.

Southwest Montana

Trip #1: The Big Hole Country

This area is dominated by high mountain peaks and big, broad river valleys. The major geographic features are the Pioneer Mountains, the Pintlar Range, the Bitterroot Mountains and the famous Big Hole River. Start at Butte and head west on Interstate 90, turning off on the road to Anaconda. Just before Anaconda, take State Highway 274 through the Deep Creek area. It offers magnificent views of the Pintlar Range. Highway 274 reaches State Highway 43 along the Big Hole River; follow 43 south toward Wisdom, where you will enter the actual valley of the Big Hole River. Take secondary road 278 to Jackson, and the Jackson Hot Springs region. Side roads lead into Twin Lakes and Miner Lakes, and the Bitterroot Mountains. From Jackson, continue on Highway 278 over Big Hole Pass, which offers an outstanding view of the valley and a great photographic spot. You can take a side trip just beyond Big Hole Pass, where a road leads to Polaris and bisects the Pioneer Mountain Range. There are accommodations in this area and it is a worthwhile place to visit. Return from Bannack across Badger Pass on Highway 278 until you reach Interstate 15, and then head for Dillon. From Dillon, follow the Interstate back to Butte. This is an outstanding photographic journey, so take plenty of time. Accommodations are available en route and although this trip could be done in one or two days without any side trips, it is better to take three to five days to do it.

Trip #2: Butte—Pipestone Pass—Virginia City

This trip starts in Butte, and offers some of Montana's most spectacular big valleys and mountain scenery. From Butte, take the scenic route over Pipestone Pass on US 10. Highway 10 intersects State Route 41; follow it south through the town of Silver Star to Twin Bridges. On the west will be the Butte Highlands and to the east rise the Tobacco Root Mountains. At Twin Bridges, go south on Highway 287 through Alder and to Nevada City and Virginia City. Virginia City was Montana's second

(Following page, above) From a viewpoint at the top of Mt. Wright, the Rocky Mountain Front Range stretches in rugged grandeur into the distance. Snow falls at these altitudes well into the summer months.
(Following page, below) A spectacular Montana sunset tints the still waters of the Flathead River, near Columbia Falls.

territorial capital and both areas have well-restored buildings of a bygone era. In the summertime, the museums and shops are open. This is an area well worth camping in and exploring thoroughly.

Trip #3: Ennis—Madison Canyon—Quake Lake Tobacco Root Mountains

At Ennis, drive south on US 287, turning east through the Madison Canyon and the site of the Madison Earthquake at Quake Lake. There is a visitors' center here explaining the earthquake. Highway 287 passes Quake Lake and follows the shore of Hebgen Lake farther east along the valley. There are some great sights for photography in this area, and it should be mentioned that this is a beautiful trip in the fall because of the many aspen and cottonwood trees that turn a magnificent golden yellow set against the snow-covered peaks of the Madison Range. Where Highway 287 meets 191, drive north through the Gallatin Valley. The Madison Range rises on the west, the Gallatin Range on the east. Follow 191 north to the junction with Secondary Route 289. Turn west for a trip through the Beartrap Canyon Primitive Area. This is a spectacular stretch of the Madison River and a beautiful canyon. Highway 289 comes out at Norris. At this point, turn north on 287, and just a short distance north of Harrison, turn west on 359. It intersects Interstate 90, which will take you back to Butte. There are many great vistas here, and also some well-marked side trips that go into the Tobacco Root Mountains. You should take time for this trip, spending a night in the Virginia City area, another one camping out in Hebgen Lake region or perhaps staying at a motel in West Yellowstone, then possibly camping again in the Bear Trap Canyon area.

(Preceding page, above) Heavy snowfall and foggy conditions create these "snow ghosts" in the Rattlesnake Mountains at the Snow Bowl Ski area near Missoula.

(Preceding page, below) Park Lake is a popular recreation spot for the people of nearby Helena.

In Closing . . .

These trips are but suggestions: they take in a representative sample of Montana's scenery and offer the photographer a chance to build an excellent collection of slides. Actually, the best time to travel most of these routes, especially in the eastern sector of the state, is in the late spring and early summer. Eastern Montana is at its best at that time of year, though it does offer excellent fall scenery, especially in the areas of the Missouri and Yellowstone Rivers. Winter travel and camping, however, is somewhat limited in most of these regions, but for those willing to endure the weather, the winters in the east are beautiful in a powerful and moving way. The western sectors of the state, however, offer outstanding scenery year around, and slightly milder winters.

No matter where you go, you can't go wrong. Montana, the Treasure State, has it all.

(Following page) Lupine blooms on the prairie in early July, while in the background thunderheads form over the Crazy Mountains.